I'm helping Mum prepa
I'm making charoset fro
wine – it tastes good! We'll put it on our seder plate for our special meal tonight.

Our seder plate helps us to tell the story of how God helped the Jews to escape from being slaves.

I'll tell you the story.

The Jews were slaves in Egypt. Pharoah, the king of Egypt, treated the slaves badly. They had to make bricks out of mud and straw to build palaces and storehouses for grain.

The Jews had to work hard. They were not free to do what they wanted. It was a time of sadness and tears.

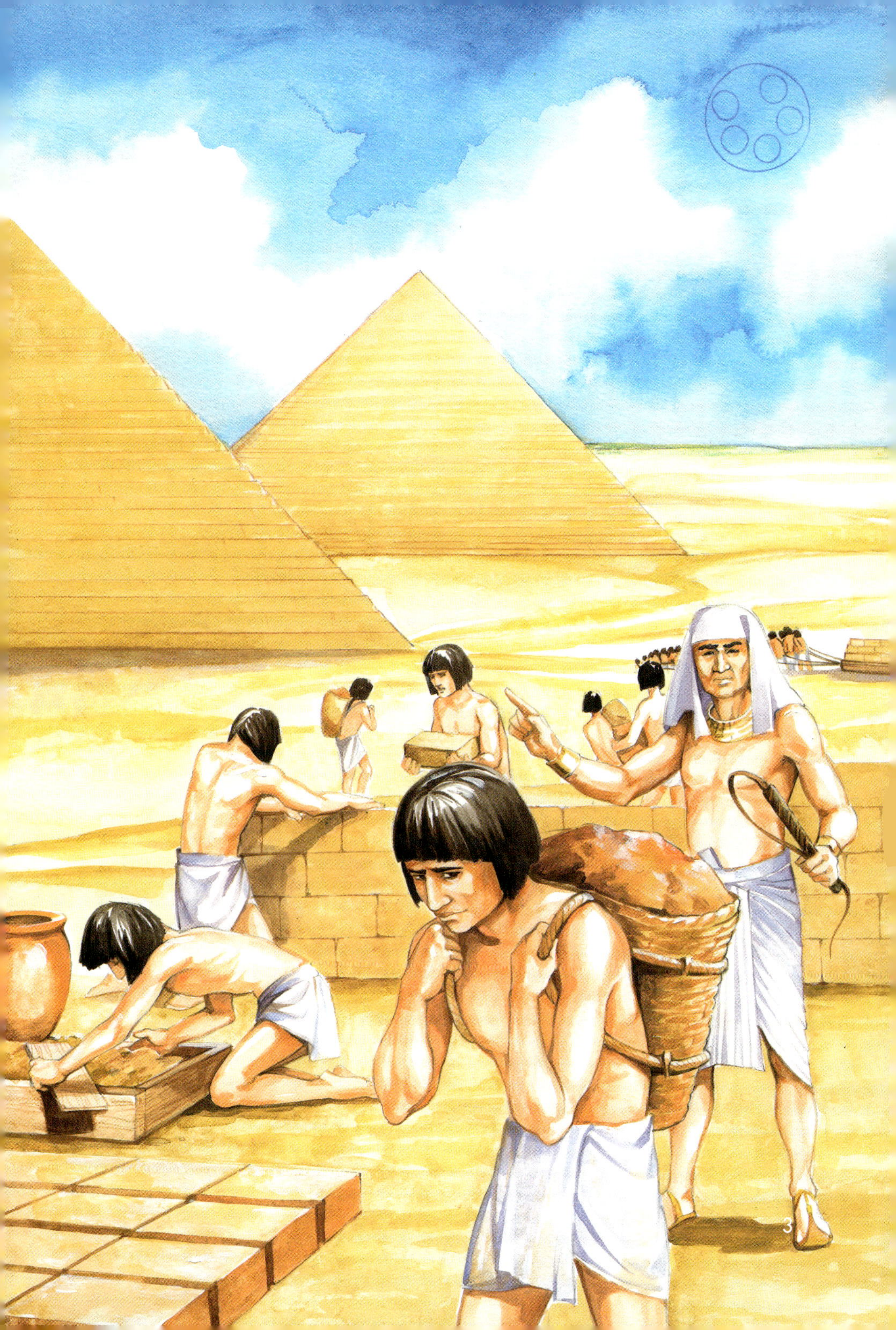

God told Moses to ask Pharoah to set the Jews free. Moses took his brother Aaron with him.

"Please let my people go," Moses asked.

At first, Pharoah said yes. But then he thought, "If I let the Jews go free, I'll have no slaves to work for me!"

So Pharoah changed his mind.

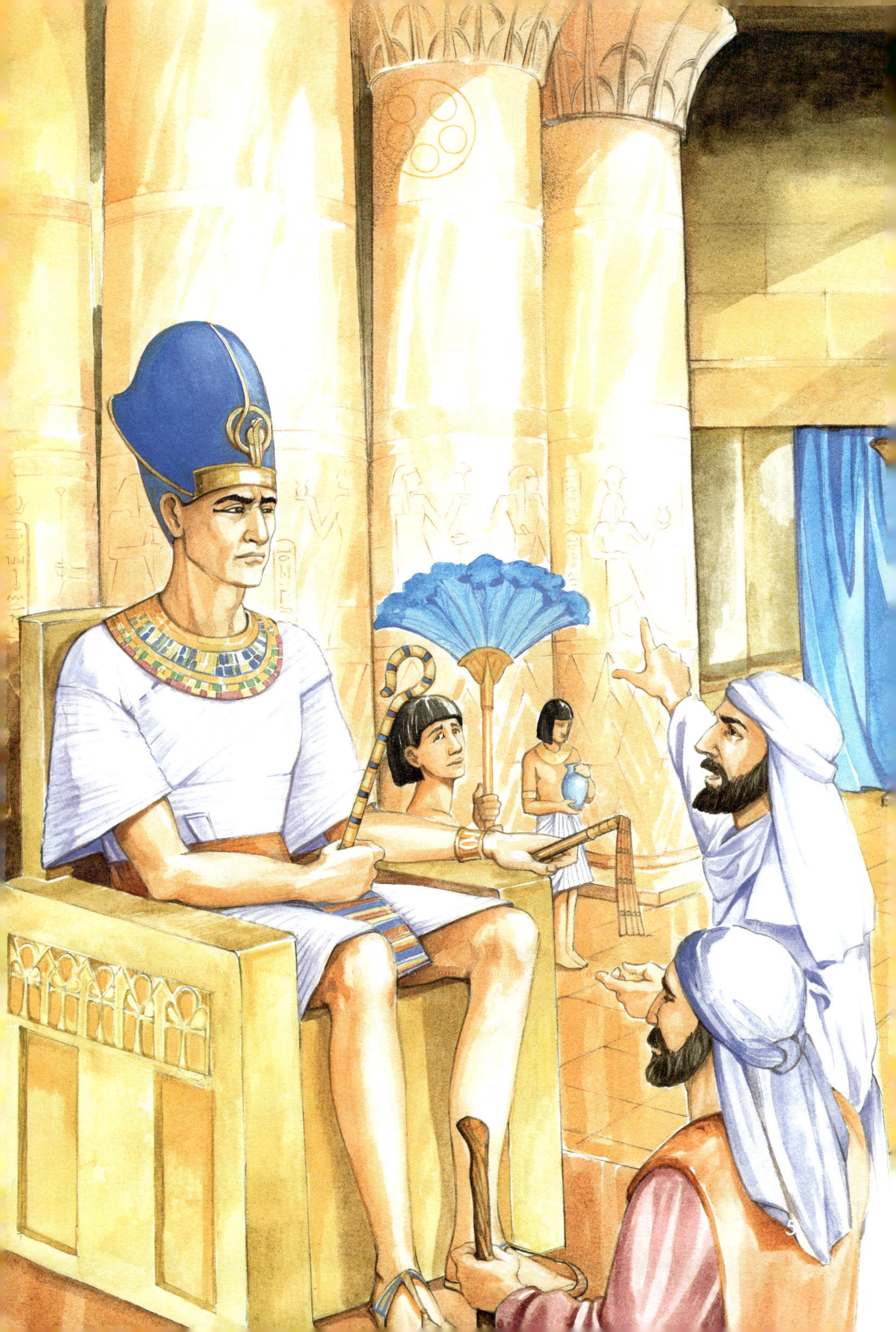

God was angry with Pharoah. He sent plagues to Egypt to remind Pharoah that he should listen to Moses.

First all the rivers turned red like blood.
Next a plague of frogs jumped into the beds and ovens of the Egyptians.
Then swarms of mosquitoes bit everyone.
Then there were swarms of horrible flies everywhere.
Then the Egyptians' cattle died.
Then all the people and animals got painful boils.
Then huge hailstones fell.
Then thousands of locusts ate all the plants and crops.
And then it was dark for three whole days.

7

When each plague came, Pharoah was scared. He told Moses that the Jews could go free.

But each time the plague stopped, Pharoah changed his mind again.

So the Jews were still slaves in Egypt. And God was angry.

There would be one more plague, the worst plague of all. But it would help to set the Jews free.

Inside back cover of Big Book, actual size

TIMES TO REMEMBER SERIES

Let My People Go
The Story of Pesach

Teacher's Notes

Artefacts for Telling the Story

- Seder plate with seder foods
- Matzot
- Bowl of salt water
- Children's Haggadah

BIG BOOKS IN THE TIMES TO REMEMBER SERIES:

- **A Birthday to Celebrate**
  A Story of Guru Nanak
  1 85175 181 5

- **A Day to Rest**
  The Story of Shabbat
  1 85175 178 5

- **Let My People Go**
  The Story of Pesach
  1 85175 209 9

- **A Row of Lights**
  The Story of Rama and Sita
  1 85175 179 3

- **The Tallest Candle**
  A Story for Christmas
  1 85175 180 7

- **Under the Bodhi Tree**
  A Story of the Buddha
  1 85175 203 X

- **A Very Special Sunday**
  A Story for Easter
  1 85175 212 9

- **Watching for the Moon**
  A Story of the Prophet Muhammad
  1 85175 206 4

Activities

Activities with a Literacy Focus

- Discuss the series of pictures on page 7. Invite individual/small groups of pupils to describe or role-play the events shown in each picture.
- Roleplay the scene when Moses asks Pharoah to let the Jews go free. Discuss the arguments which might persuade Pharoah.
- Discuss the characters of Moses and Pharoah. How are their characters displayed through their actions?
- Make a collage or draw Moses and Pharoah. Add speech bubbles to illustrate the character of each.
- Set a table for the seder meal. If a seder plate is not available, the items could be set out on one large plate or in small ramekin dishes. First make a list of all the items required: a lamb bone, lettuce, parsley, a roasted egg, horseradish, charoset, matzot, salt water. Then lay the table with a white cloth or paper and display the items.
- Taste some of the foods on the seder plate (not the egg or bone) and find words to describe the horseradish, charoset and matzot. Some Jewish families begin their seder meal by eating a hardboiled egg in salt water.
- Look at the illustrations which match the text in a children's Haggadah.

Additional Activities

- Think/talk about the times when the children:
  (a) sit together and tell special or favourite stories,
  (b) share a celebration meal.
- Discuss how Moses might have felt asking the powerful Pharoah to let the people go free. How did he have the courage to ask? (Remember: God had told him to go to Pharoah.)
- Invite a Jewish parent/visitor to describe how s/he prepares for and celebrates Pesach.
- Think about the people who have to leave their country and become refugees today.
- Make some charoset. Mix one sweet, chopped apple with about a tablespoon of finely chopped or minced nuts (walnuts are best) and half a level teaspoon of ground cinnamon. Moisten with red grape juice (instead of wine) until of the consistency of mortar. Sweeten with sugar or honey if necessary.

Assessing Learning in RE

After reading the story and engaging in the follow-up activities:

- Can the children retell the story of how God helped the Jews to escape from being slaves?
- Can they talk about Moses and Pharoah as examples of 'good' and 'bad' characters in the story?
- Can they explain why the story of Moses is a special story for Jews to remember at Pesach?
- Can they explain why Jews have bitter herbs and charoset on their seder plate and a bowl of salt water and matzot on their seder table?
- Can they talk about a festival or celebration when they eat special food?

Copyright ©2000 Lynne Broadbent and John Logan

… MEMBER SERIES

Let My People Go
The Story of Pesach

Teacher's Notes

There are two parts to *Let My People Go*: the celebration of the festival of Pesach (Passover) and the retelling of the story of the escape of the Jews from slavery in Egypt.

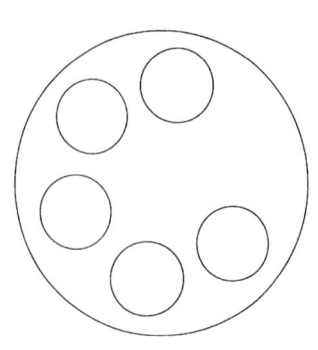

A drawing of a seder plate is hidden in each of the illustrations on pages 3, 5, 7, 9, 11 and 13.

The Story

The story of the Exodus – how God, through Moses, led the Jews from slavery in Egypt to freedom in the Promised Land – is told in the Torah and can be found in the Christian Bible in the Book of Exodus. The Torah consists of the five 'Books of Moses' (also the first five books of the Christian Bible) and is the most important part of Jewish scripture.

When retelling the Exodus story, it would be more correct to use the term 'Hebrews' or 'Israelites', rather than referring to the slaves as 'Jews'. However, in this book for young children, the term 'Jews' is used throughout, both to avoid confusion and to reinforce the link with modern Jewish practice.

Page 2 The Jews had been welcomed into Egypt by a previous Pharaoh after Joseph had saved the country from famine by warning the Pharaoh to build storehouses for corn during seven years of plenty. Now, about 300 years later, the Jews had grown in number and the new Pharaoh saw them as a threat. As a result he made them slaves.

Page 4 God had spoken to Moses through a burning bush and told him to go to Pharaoh and ask for the Jews to be freed. Moses did not feel confident speaking to Pharaoh, so he took Aaron with him.

Page 6 It is important here for the children not to see God as a 'magician' who conveniently created the plagues. They need to understand that the Jews were being cruelly treated. Pharaoh knew this, and when the disasters happened, he himself believed that they were a punishment from God. Some people understand the plagues to be a series of natural and linked disasters stemming from the River Nile overflowing its banks and being coloured red by the alluvial soil, thus leading to the frogs, gnats, sickness and death.

Page 10 Moses told the Jews to cook a young lamb in bitter herbs. The people made their bread in a hurry so they did not put any yeast in it, and it did not rise.

Page 14 At the seder meal, Jewish families retell the story of how God through Moses led the people out of slavery. It is a time to celebrate the freedom of the Jewish people and to remember all those who are not free to live life as they would choose.

The Festival

The festival of Pesach (Passover) is celebrated by Jews each year in March or April. The exact date can be found in the annual Shap Calendar of Festivals (available from The National Society's RE Centre, 36 Causton Street, London SW1P 4AU; tel. 020 7932 1190, email: nsrec@dial.pipex.com).

The festival commemorates the Exodus, the story of God, through Moses, leading the Jews from slavery in Egypt to freedom in the Promised Land. It is celebrated for eight days and a highlight is the special meal, the seder meal, eaten on the first and sometimes second night, usually in a family home. During the meal, the foods on the seder plate (see page 15) provide prompts for telling the story:

- **Charoset** – this sweet mixture of chopped apple and nuts, mixed together with cinnamon and wine, is a reminder of the mortar used by the Jewish slaves to build the cities.
- **Bitter herbs** (usually horseradish) – a symbol of the bitter times as slaves in Egypt.
- **Shankbone of lamb** – a reminder of the lamb that was eaten before the Jews began their long journey to freedom.
- **Roast egg** – a hardboiled egg, with its shell 'roasted' or scorched by a flame, is a symbol of sacrificial offerings made in the Temple.
- **Parsley and/or lettuce** – symbols of spring.

A bowl of **salt water** on the table is a reminder of the tears or the sweat of the slaves. **Matzot** (singular: matzah – unleavened 'bread', i.e. containing no yeast) are a reminder of the unleavened bread quickly made before the escape from Egypt. Before Pesach begins, the family has to clean the house thoroughly to make sure that nothing containing yeast remains in it. Anything containing a raising agent is thrown out or given away. For the eight days of the festival, matzot are eaten instead of bread.

Copyright ©2000 Lynne Broadbent and John Logan

9

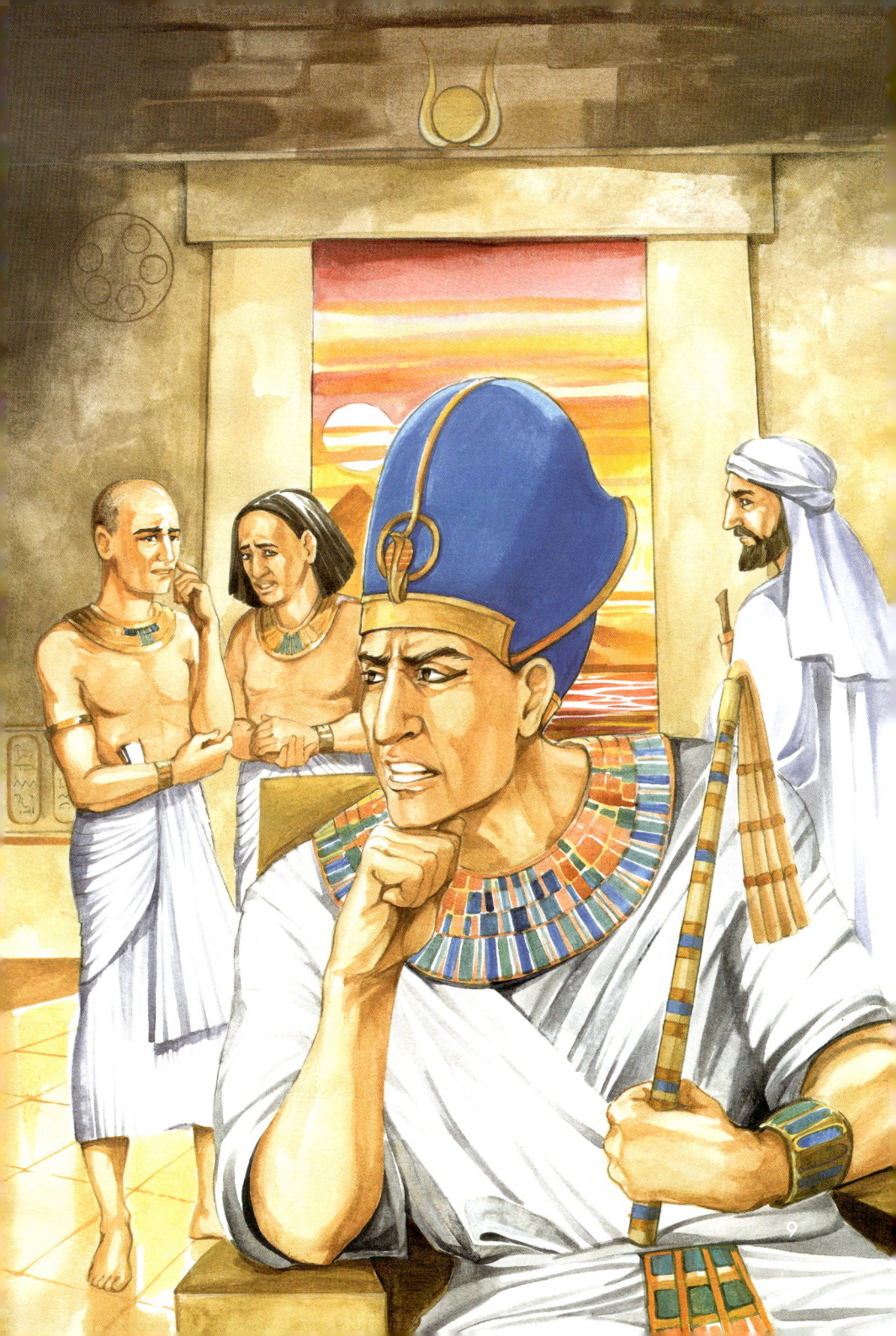

Moses told the Jews to get ready for a long journey. They made a special meal of lamb roasted with bitter herbs and flat bread. This bread had to be made so quickly that it didn't have time to rise.

That night, something terrible happened in the homes of the Egyptians. In every home, the firstborn, oldest child and the firstborn of every animal died.

While the Egyptian families cried, Moses led all the Jews out of Egypt.

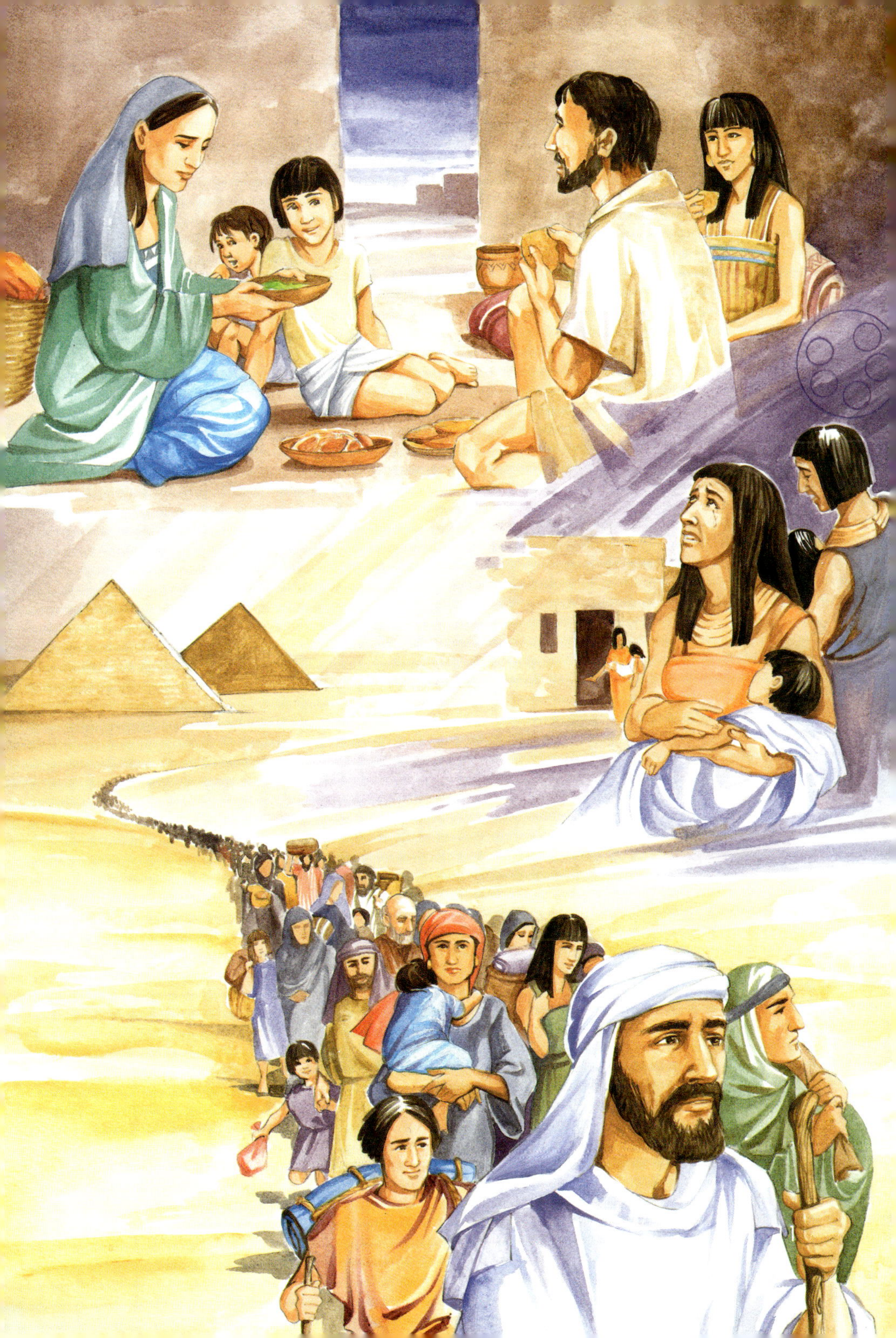

Moses led the Jews on a very long journey across rivers and deserts until they reached a country where they could stay, a country they could call home. The Jews built new cities and homes for themselves.

The Jews were no longer slaves – they were free.

13

At Pesach, we remember how God set the Jews free. The bitter herbs on our seder plate remind us of the bitter times when the Jews were slaves. A bowl of salt water reminds us of the sweat of hard work and the tears of the slaves.

We eat matzot, which taste like cream crackers, to remind us of the flat bread which did not have time to rise. And best of all, we eat charoset to remind us of the sweet times when the slaves were free and could build their homes again.

מי מלח
salt water

ביצה
roast egg

זרוע
roast bone

כרפס
Parsley

מרור
bitter herb

חזרת
lettuce

חרוסת
charoset

15

Can you tell a story about Pesach?

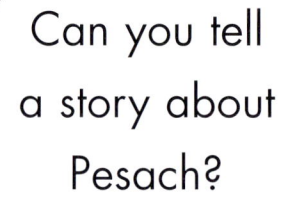